# CONTENTS

1C

# This Is Big

## Learn

Words

**A** Listen and repeat. Then chant. ▶ 🎧03 🎧04

**B** Listen and repeat. ▶ 🎧05

**C** Stick and say.

This is big.

**2** small

**1** big

**3** long

**4** short

**5** new

**6** old

**8** cold

**7** hot

**Listen, find, and draw.** 06

**1** ◯   **2** △   **3** ▢

# Let's Listen

**A** Listen and sing. Then match. ▶ 🔊07

## This Is Big

Big, big. This is big.

Small, small. This is small.

Hot, hot. This is hot.

Cold, cold. This is cold.

**B** Listen and circle. Then say. 🎧08

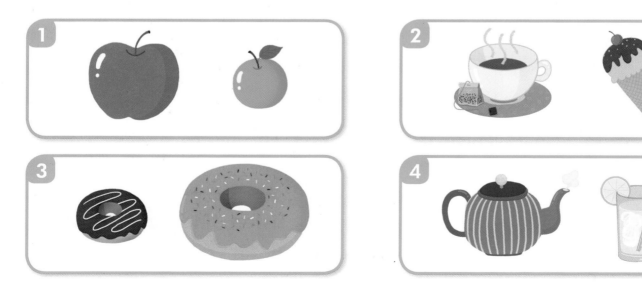

1
2
3
4

# Let's Talk

A **Listen and stick. Then say.** 09

1 small

2 big

3 new

This is _____.

4 old

5 long

6 short

# Words

## A Trace and circle.

**1** big

**2** small

**3** long
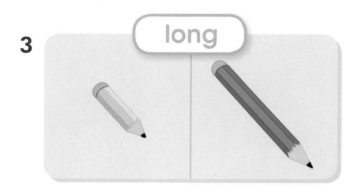

**4** short

**5** new

**6** old

**7** hot

**8** cold

# Subject Link

**A** Write and say.

big    short
long   small

**1**

This is _____.

**2**

This is _____.

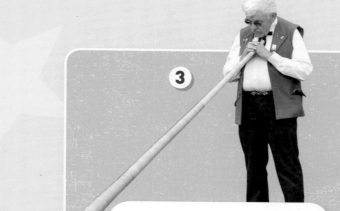

**3**

This is _____.

**4**

This is _____.

**B** Connect and write.

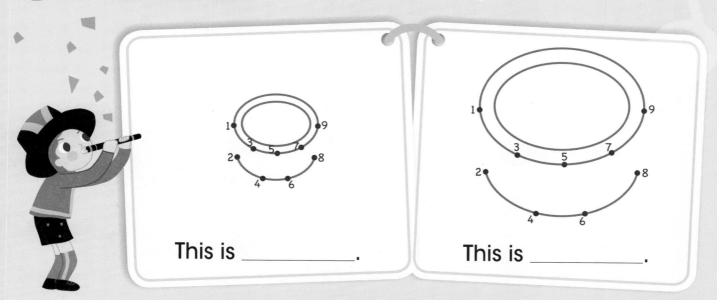

This is _____.

This is _____.

**Ⓐ Listen and number.** 🎧 10

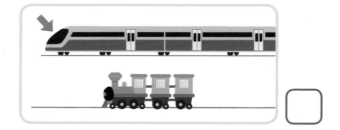

**Ⓑ Listen and circle.** 🎧 11

1   big   ✂   small

2   long   ✂   short

3   old   ✂   new

4   hot   ✂   cold

**Ⓒ Listen and choose.** 🎧 12

1

ⓐ
ⓑ

2

ⓐ
ⓑ

## Ⓐ Listen, say, and write. 🎧13

**1**

p

☐en          ☐ig          ☐izza

**2**

b

☐ee          ☐ed          ☐ox

## Ⓑ Listen and circle. 🎧14

**1** p  b          **2** p  b          **3** p  b

## Ⓒ Circle and write.

**1**

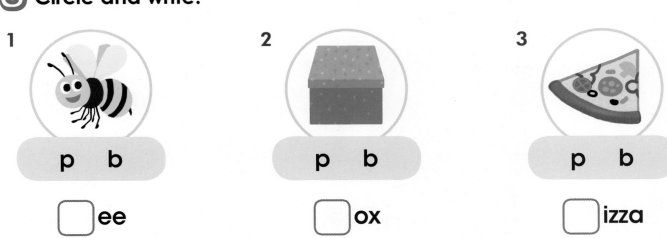

p  b          p  b          p  b

☐ee          ☐ox          ☐izza

# UNIT 2 That's a Grasshopper

## Learn

Words

A Listen and repeat. Then chant.

B Listen and repeat.

C Stick and say.

1 a spider

2 a grasshopper

3 an ant

That's a grasshopper.

10

**4** a bee

**5** a butterfly

**6** a beetle

**7** a dragonfly

**8** a ladybug

Quiz

Listen, find, and draw.

**1** ◯  **2** △  **3** ☐

# Let's Listen

**A** Listen and sing. Then match. ▶ 🎧20

## That's a Butterfly

Look! That's a butterfly. Butterfly.

That's a dragonfly. Dragonfly.

Look! That's a ladybug. Ladybug.

That's a grasshopper. Grasshopper.

**B** Listen and stick. Then say. 🎧21

1 Sticker

2 Sticker

3 Sticker

4 Sticker

# Let's Talk

a bee ◯

a beetle ◯

a spider ◯

a butterfly ◯

a dragonfly ◯

an ant ◯

That's _____.

# Words

## A Match and write.

**1**

ant

bee

beetle

ladybug

butterfly

dragonfly

grasshopper

spider

**2**

**3**

**4**

**5**

**6**

**7**

**8**

# Subject Link

bee  spider  beetle
butterfly  dragonfly

**A** Write and say.

1. That's a _____.

2. That's a _____.

3. That's a _____.

4. That's a _____.

5. That's a _____.

**B** Stick and write.

That's a _____.

# Check-Up

## A Listen and mark ○ or ✕. 🎧23

1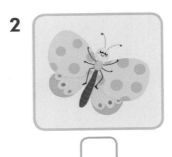

2

3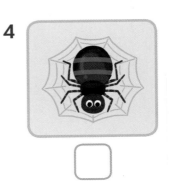

4

## B Listen and match. 🎧24

1 •

2 •

3 •

4 •

• grasshopper

• bee

• ladybug

• beetle

## C Listen and choose. Then say. 🎧25

1

ⓐ

ⓑ

2

ⓐ

ⓑ

16

**Ⓐ Listen, say, and write.** 🎧26

**1**

t

☐ent    ☐iger    ☐urtle

**2**

d

☐og    ☐oll    ☐esk

**Ⓑ Listen and match.** 🎧27

① •    ② •    ③ •

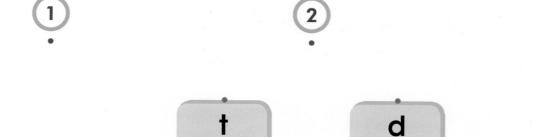

t    d

**Ⓒ Look and write.**

**1**    **2**    **3**

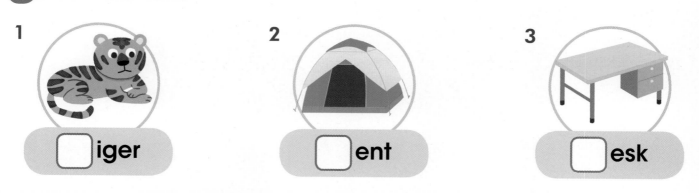

☐iger    ☐ent    ☐esk

# Review 1

**A** Listen and circle. 🎧 28

**1**

**2**

**3**

**4**

**5**

**6**

**7**

**8**

**B** **Read and check.**

1

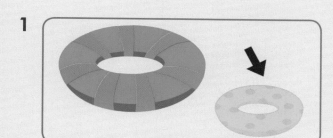

- [ ] This is big.
- [ ] This is small.

2

- [ ] This is new.
- [ ] This is old.

3

- [ ] That's an ant.
- [ ] That's a beetle.

4

- [ ] This is long.
- [ ] This is short.

5

- [ ] That's a grasshopper.
- [ ] That's a ladybug.

6

- [ ] That's a bee.
- [ ] That's a dragonfly.

7

- [ ] That's a spider.
- [ ] That's a butterfly.

8

- [ ] This is hot.
- [ ] This is cold.

# I Like My Red Scarf

## Learn

Words

(A) Listen and repeat. Then chant. ▶ 🎧30 🎧31

(B) Listen and repeat. ▶ 🎧32

(C) Stick and say.

I like my scarf.
I like my red scarf.

② black hat

① red scarf

③ green vest

④ blue coat

**5** red **shirt**

**6** green **sweater**

**7** black **boots**

**8** blue **shoes**

Quiz

Listen, find, and draw. 🎧33

**1** ◯  **2** △  **3** ▢

# Let's Listen

**A** Listen and sing. Then match.

## I Like My Yellow Coat

Yellow coat. I like my yellow coat.

Red sweater. I like my red sweater.

Green vest. I like my green vest.

Blue hat. I like my blue hat.

**B** Listen and stick. Then say.

1
2
3
4

22

# Let's Talk

green shirt

black coat

yellow scarf

blue boots

red shoes

I like my _____.

# Words

**A** Look and write.

| scarf | vest | hat | coat |
|-------|------|-----|------|
| boots | shoes | shirt | sweater |

24

# Subject Link

scarf  shirt
hat  coat

**A** Write and say.

I like my white _____.

I like my yellow _____.

I like my green _____.

I like my black _____.

**B** Color, choose, and write.

I like my _____ _____.

**A** Listen and number. 🎧37

**B** Listen and circle. 🎧38

1
red shirt
red scarf

2
yellow shoes
yellow hat

3
white coat
white vest

4
black shoes
black boots

**C** Listen and choose. Then say. 🎧39

1

a
b

2

a
b

**Ⓐ Listen, say, and write.** 🎧40

**1**

c / k

☐ oat    ☐ at    ☐ ite

**2**

g

☐ oat    ☐ ame    ☐ irl

**Ⓑ Listen and circle.** 🎧41

**1** g / c    **2** k / g    **3** k / g    **4** g / k

**Ⓒ Look and write.**

**1**

☐ at

**2**

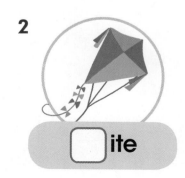

☐ ite

**3**

☐ oat

# I Can Play the Piano

## Learn

**Words**

**A** Listen and repeat. Then chant. ▶ 43 44

**B** Listen and repeat. ▶ 45

**C** Stick and say.

I can play the piano.

1 violin

2 flute

3 piano

4 recorder

**5** drums

**7** trumpet

**6** guitar

Quiz

**Listen, find, and draw.** 🎧 46

**1** ◯  **2** △  **3** ☐

# Let's Listen

**A** Listen and sing. Then match. ▶ 47

## I Can Play the Trumpet

I can play the trumpet.

I can play the flute.

I can play the violin.

I can play the recorder.

**B** Listen and match. Then say. 48

①      ②      ③      ④

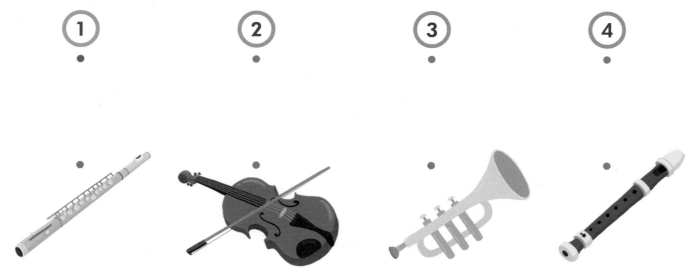

# Let's Talk

**Listen and number. Then say.** 49

I can play the _____.

drums

piano

trumpet

guitar

violin

recorder

# Words

**Ⓐ Look and write.**

| piano | flute | violin | guitar |
| drums | trumpet | recorder |

**1**

**2**

**3**

**4**

**5**

**6**

**7**

# Subject Link

**guitar   trumpet
flute   violin   drums**

**A** **Write and say.**

 I can play the _____.

 I can play the _____.

 I can play the _____.

 I can play the _____.

 I can play the _____.

**B** **What can you play? Circle and write.**

I can play the _____.

**Ⓐ Listen and match.** 50

1

2

3

4

**Ⓑ Listen and number.** 51

| guitar | recorder | drums | piano |

○  ○  ○  ○

**Ⓒ Listen and choose. Then say.** 52

1

ⓐ ⓑ

2

ⓐ ⓑ

# Phonics

## A Listen, say, and write. 🎧53

1

**S**

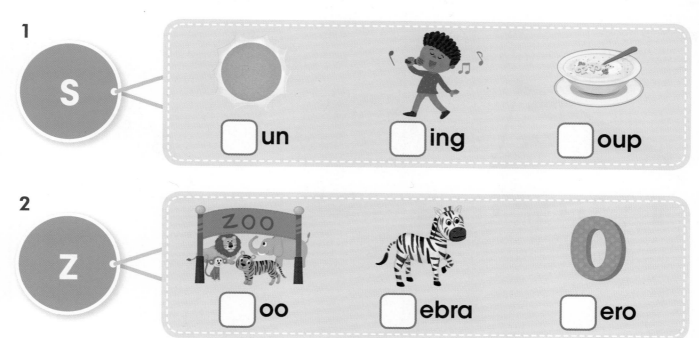

☐ un          ☐ ing          ☐ oup

2

**Z**

☐ oo          ☐ ebra          ☐ ero

## B Listen and circle. 🎧54

1   S / Z          2   S / Z          3   S / Z

## C Look and match.

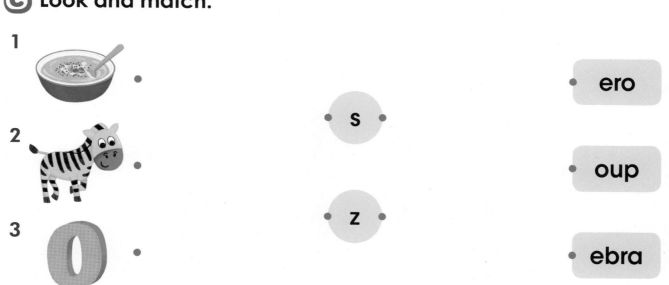

1

2

3

S

Z

ero

oup

ebra

**A** Listen and number. 55

**Ⓑ Read and circle.**

**1** I like my red coat.

**2** I like my white shoes.

**3** I like my green sweater.

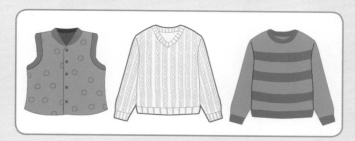

**4** I like my yellow vest.

**5** I can play the flute.

**6** I can play the recorder.

**7** I can play the piano.

**8** I can play the violin.

## Learn

**Words**

**A** Listen and repeat. Then chant. ▶ 57 58

**B** Listen and repeat. ▶ 59

**C** Stick and say.

1 sky

3 sun

2 rainbow

Look at the lake.

4 lake

5 flower

**6** star

**7** moon

**8** tree

Quiz

**Listen, find, and draw.** 🎧 60

**1** ◯  **2** △  **3** ▢

# Let's Listen

**A** Listen and sing. Then match.

### Look at the Sky

Look! Look at the sky. Sky!

Look at the rainbow. Rainbow!

Look! Look at the lake. Lake!

Look at the sun. Sun!

**B** Listen and number. Then say.

# Let's Talk

A Listen and stick. Then say. 🎧 63

1 star

2 moon

3 flower

4 tree

5 rainbow

6 lake

Look at the _____.

# Words

## A Circle and write.

**1**

sun

rainbow

_____

**2**
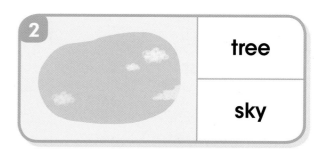

tree

sky

_____

**3**

star

flower

_____

**4**
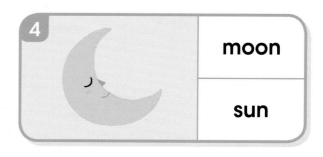

moon

sun

_____

**5**
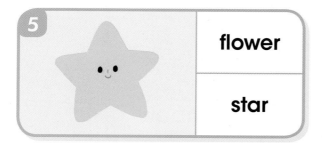

flower

star

_____

**6**

rainbow

sun

_____

**7**

tree

sky

_____

**8**

moon

lake

_____

# Subject Link

tree   moon
sky   star

## A Write and say.

Look at the _____.

Look at the _____.

Look at the _____.

Look at the _____.

## B Color, choose, and write.

Look at the _____.

# Check-Up

## A Listen and check. 🎧64

1

2

3

4

## B Listen and circle. 🎧65

| 1 | sun | tree |

| 2 | tree | star |

| 3 | lake | flower |

| 4 | rainbow | moon |

## C Listen and choose. Then say. 🎧66

1
ⓐ
ⓑ

2
ⓐ
ⓑ

44

**(A) Listen, say, and write.** 🎧 67

1

**f**

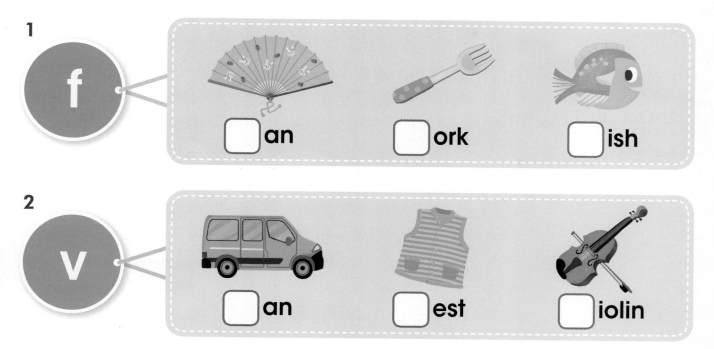

☐ an    ☐ ork    ☐ ish

2

**v**

☐ an    ☐ est    ☐ iolin

**(B) Listen and circle.** 🎧 68

1  f | v      2  f | v      3  f | v

**(C) Look and write.**

1

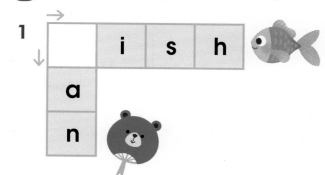

| | i | s | h |
| a |
| n |

2

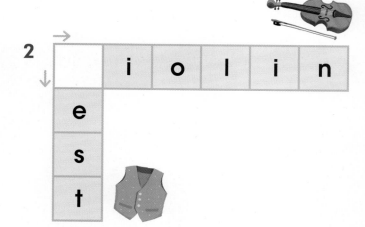

| | i | o | l | i | n |
| e |
| s |
| t |

# I'm a Police Officer

## Learn

Words

**A** Listen and repeat. Then chant. ▶ 🎧70 🎧71

**B** Listen and repeat. ▶ 🎧72

**C** Stick and say.

1 cook

2 singer

3 teacher

4 police officer

I'm a police officer.

5 pilot

6 doctor

7 nurse

8 firefighter

Quiz

Listen, find, and draw. 🎧 73

1 ◯  2 △  3 ▢

# Let's Listen

**A** Listen and sing. Then match. ▶ 74

I'm a Police Officer

I'm a police officer, police officer.

I'm a singer, singer. Yeah!

I'm a firefighter, firefighter.

I'm a nurse, nurse. Yeah!

**B** Listen and match. Then say. 75

1

2

3

4

# Let's Talk

Listen, number, and match. Then say. 🎧 76

I'm a _____.

cook

police officer

teacher

firefighter

pilot

doctor

# Words

## A Look and write.

| cook | doctor | nurse | pilot |
|------|--------|-------|-------|
| singer | teacher | firefighter | police officer |

# Subject Link

**A** Stick, write, and say.

| police officer | doctor |
| firefighter | teacher |

**1**

I'm a _____.

**2**

I'm a _____.

**3**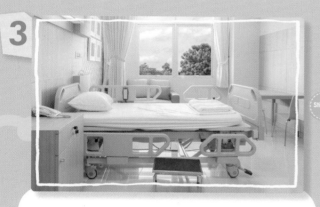

I'm a _____.

**4**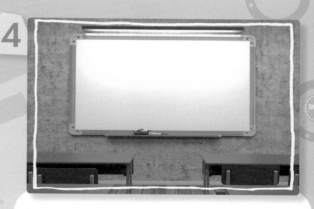

I'm a _____.

**B** Stick and write.

I'm a _____.

# Check-Up

## A Listen and number. 🎧77

 ☐

 ☐

 ☐

 ☐

## B Listen and match. 🎧78

1 •     2 •     3 •     4 •

firefighter    teacher    cook    doctor

## C Listen and choose. Then say. 🎧79

1

ⓐ
ⓑ

2

ⓐ
ⓑ

**Ⓐ Listen, say, and write.** 🎧80

1

m

☐ilk    ☐ouse    ☐onkey

2

n

☐et    ☐ine    ☐ose

**Ⓑ Listen and circle.** 🎧81

1    m   n        2    m   n        3    m   n

**Ⓒ Look, match, and write.**

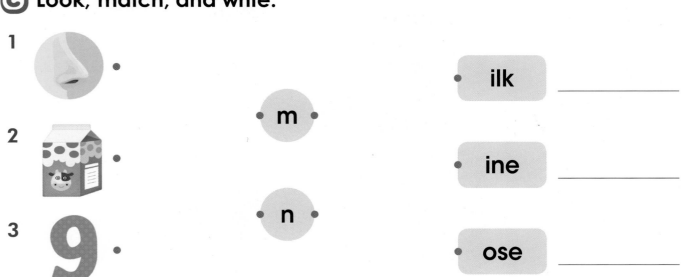

1    •

• m •

2    •

• n •

3    •

• ilk  _____

• ine  _____

• ose  _____

**A** Listen and match. 🎧 82

1 •     2 •     3 •     4 •

5 •     6 •     7 •     8 •

## Ⓑ Read and number.

1 I'm a doctor.

2 Look at the moon.

3 Look at the sky.

4 I'm a teacher.

5 I'm a firefighter.

6 Look at the lake.

7 I'm a pilot.

8 Look at the star.

# Learn

Words
**A** Listen and repeat. Then chant. ▶
**B** Listen and repeat. ▶
**C** Stick and say.

1 study

2 draw

3 eat

Let's go.

Okay.

4 go

5 read

6 help

7 clean

8 play

Quiz

Listen, find, and draw. 🎧87

1 ◯   2 △   3 ▢

# Let's Listen

**A** Listen and sing. Then match. ▶️ 🎧88

Let's Play

Eat, eat. Let's eat. Okay.

Play, play. Let's play.

Draw, draw. Let's draw. Okay.

Go, go. Let's go. Okay.

**B** Listen and stick. Then say. 🎧89

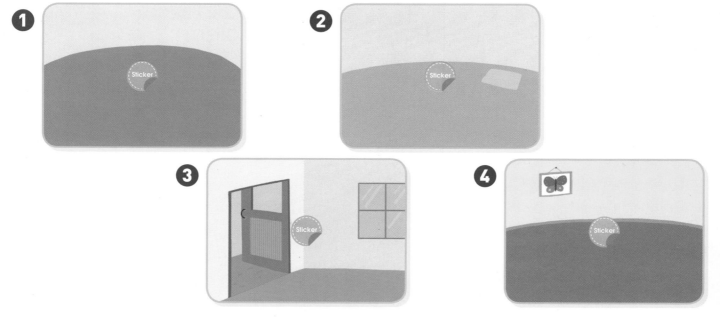

1

2

3

4

# Let's Talk

# Words

**A** Match and trace.

| go | read | play | help |
|----|------|------|------|

| study | clean | draw | eat |
|-------|-------|------|-----|

# Subject Link

play    read
study   eat

## A Match, write, and say.

**1**

Let's _____.

**2**

Let's _____.

**3**

Let's _____.

**4**

Let's _____.

## B Circle and write.

Let's _____.

Okay.

# Check-Up

## A) Listen and check. 🎧91

**1**

**2**

**3**

**4**

## B) Listen and number. 🎧92

| help | eat | draw | read |
| --- | --- | --- | --- |
| ◯ | ◯ | ◯ | ◯ |

## C) Listen and choose. Then say. 🎧93

**1**

ⓐ

ⓑ

**2**

ⓐ

ⓑ

**Ⓐ Listen, say, and write.** 🎧94

1 **l**

☐ion    ☐emon    ☐amp

2 **r**

☐ed    ☐abbit    ☐ing

**Ⓑ Listen and match.** 🎧95

① •    ② •    ③ •

l    r

**Ⓒ Look and write.**

1

☐ion

2
☐amp

3
☐ed

# It's on the Sofa

## Learn

Words

(A) Listen and repeat. Then chant. ▶ 🎧97 🎧98

(B) Listen and repeat. ▶ 🎧99

(C) Stick and say.

**1** sofa

**2** wardrobe

Where's my robot?

**3** table

It's on the sofa.

**4** bookcase

**5** desk

**6** chair

**7** bed

Quiz

**Listen, find, and draw.** 🎧100

**1** ◯  **2** △  **3** ▢

# Let's Listen

**A** Listen and sing. Then match. ▶ 101

## It's on the Sofa

Where's my ball? Where's my ball?

It's on the sofa. It's on the chair.

Where's my ball? Where's my ball?

It's on the table. It's on the bookcase.

**B** Listen and stick. Then ask and answer. 102

# Let's Talk

**Listen and number. Then ask and answer.** 103

desk

wardrobe

bed

chair

sofa

table

Where's my truck?

It's on the _____.

# Words

## A Match and trace.

bookcase

table

desk

chair

bed

sofa

wardrobe

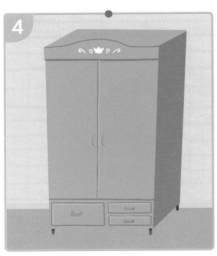

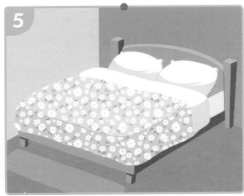

# Subject Link

bed  chair  table

**A** Stick, write, and say.

It's on the _____.

It's on the _____.

Where's my ball?

It's on the _____.

**B** Finish the picture. Then stick and write.

Where's my ball?

It's on the _____.

**Ⓐ Listen and mark ○ or ✗.** (104)

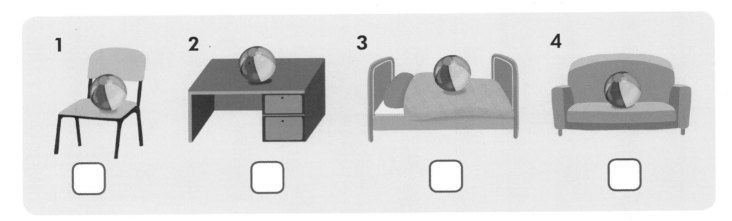

1  2  3  4

**Ⓑ Listen and circle.** (105)

| 1 | table | wardrobe |
| --- | --- | --- |

| 2 | bookcase | wardrobe |
| --- | --- | --- |

| 3 | sofa | desk |
| --- | --- | --- |

| 4 | chair | bed |
| --- | --- | --- |

**Ⓒ Listen and choose. Then ask and answer.** (106)

1

ⓐ ⓑ

2

ⓐ ⓑ

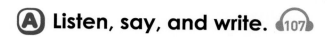

## Phonics

### A Listen, say, and write. 🎧107

**1**

**w**

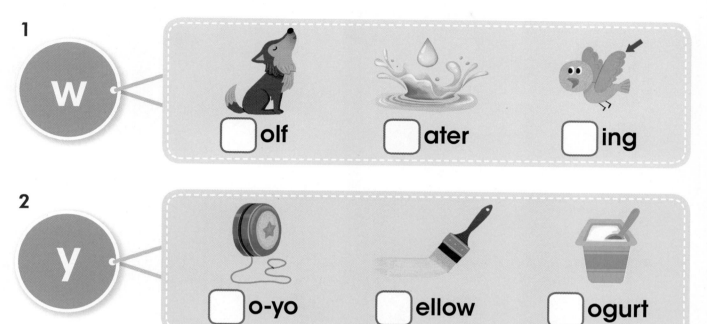

☐olf    ☐ater    ☐ing

**2**

**y**

☐o-yo    ☐ellow    ☐ogurt

### B Listen and circle. 🎧108

1  | w | y |

2  | w | y |

3  | w | y |

### C Circle and write.

**1**

| w   y |

☐ing

**2**

| w   y |

☐o-yo

**3**

| w   y |

☐ellow

**A** Listen and number. 🎧109

## B Read and write the letters.

 Let's study.

 Okay.

1 Let's study.

2 Let's draw.

3 Let's play.

4 Let's read.

5 It's on the bookcase.

6 It's on the bed.

7 It's on the wardrobe.

8 It's on the sofa.

 Where's my ball?

# Word List 1C

## Unit 1  This Is Big

bed _____

bee _____

big _____

box _____

cold _____

hot _____

long _____

new _____

old _____

pen _____

pig _____

pizza _____

short _____

small _____

## Unit 2  That's a Grasshopper

ant _____

bee _____

beetle _____

butterfly _____

desk _____

dog _____

doll _____

dragonfly _____

grasshopper _____

ladybug _____

spider _____

tent _____

tiger _____

turtle _____

## Unit 3  I Like My Red Scarf

boots _____

cat _____

coat _____

game _____

girl _____

goat _____

hat _____

kite _____

scarf _____

shirt _____

shoes _____

sweater _____

vest _____

## Unit 4  I Can Play the Piano

drums _____

flute _____

guitar _____

piano _____

recorder _____

sing _____

soup _____

sun _____

trumpet _____

violin _____

zebra _____

zero _____

zoo _____

## Unit 5 Look at the Lake

fan _____

fish _____

flower _____

fork _____

lake _____

moon _____

rainbow _____

sky _____

star _____

sun _____

tree _____

van _____

vest _____

violin _____

## Unit 6 I'm a Police Officer

cook _____

doctor _____

firefighter _____

milk _____

monkey _____

mouse _____

net _____

nine _____

nose _____

nurse _____

pilot _____

police officer _____

singer _____

teacher _____

## Unit 7 Let's Go

clean _____

draw _____

eat _____

go _____

help _____

lamp _____

lemon _____

lion _____

play _____

rabbit _____

read _____

red _____

ring _____

study _____

## Unit 8 It's on the Sofa

bed _____

bookcase _____

chair _____

desk _____

sofa _____

table _____

wardrobe _____

water _____

wing _____

wolf _____

yellow _____

yogurt _____

yo-yo _____

# Syllabus 1C

## Unit 1  This Is Big

| Structure | Vocabulary | | Phonics | Subject Link |
|---|---|---|---|---|
| This is big. | big | new | Consonants **p**, **b** | Music |
| | small | old | pen, pig, pizza | |
| | long | hot | bee, bed, box | |
| | short | cold | | |

## Unit 2  That's a Grasshopper

| Structure | Vocabulary | | Phonics | Subject Link |
|---|---|---|---|---|
| That's a grasshopper. | spider | butterfly | Consonants **t**, **d** | Art |
| That's an ant. | grasshopper | beetle | tent, tiger, turtle | |
| | ant | dragonfly | dog, doll, desk | |
| | bee | ladybug | | |
| **Review 1** | | | | |

## Unit 3  I Like My Red Scarf

| Structure | Vocabulary | | Phonics | Subject Link |
|---|---|---|---|---|
| I like my scarf. | scarf | shirt | Consonants **c/k**, **g** | Reading |
| I like my red scarf. | hat | sweater | coat, cat, kite | |
| | vest | shoes | goat, game, girl | |
| | coat | boots | | |

## Unit 4  I Can Play the Piano

| Structure | Vocabulary | | Phonics | Subject Link |
|---|---|---|---|---|
| I can play the piano. | violin | drums | Consonants **s**, **z** | Music |
| | flute | guitar | sun, sing, soup | |
| | piano | trumpet | zoo, zebra, zero | |
| | recorder | | | |
| **Review 2** | | | | |

## Unit 5  Look at the Lake

| Structure | Vocabulary | | Phonics | Subject Link |
|---|---|---|---|---|
| Look at the lake. | sky | flower | Consonants f, v | Art |
| | rainbow | star | fan, fork, fish | |
| | sun | moon | van, vest, violin | |
| | lake | tree | | |

## Unit 6  I'm a Police Officer

| Structure | Vocabulary | | Phonics | Subject Link |
|---|---|---|---|---|
| I'm a police officer. | cook | pilot | Consonants m, n | Social Studies |
| | singer | doctor | milk, mouse, monkey | |
| | teacher | nurse | net, nine, nose | |
| | police officer | firefighter | | |
| Review 3 | | | | |

## Unit 7  Let's Go

| Structure | Vocabulary | | Phonics | Subject Link |
|---|---|---|---|---|
| Let's go. | study | read | Consonants l, r | Social Studies |
| Okay. | draw | help | lion, lemon, lamp | |
| | eat | clean | red, rabbit, ring | |
| | go | play | | |

## Unit 8  It's on the Sofa

| Structure | Vocabulary | | Phonics | Subject Link |
|---|---|---|---|---|
| Where's my robot? | sofa | desk | Consonants w, y | Art |
| It's on the sofa. | wardrobe | chair | wolf, water, wing | |
| | table | bed | yo-yo, yellow, yogurt | |
| | bookcase | | | |
| Review 4 | | | | |

Unit **1**

Unit **1**

Unit **2**

Unit **2**

Unit **1**

Unit **1**

Unit **2**

Unit **2**

Unit **1**

Unit **1**

Unit **2**

Unit **2**

Unit **1**

Unit **1**

Unit **2**

Unit **2**

| | Unit 1 | Unit 1 |
|---|---|---|
| **short** | **long** | **small** | **big** |

| | Unit 2 | Unit 1 | Unit 1 |
|---|---|---|---|
| **cold** | **hot** | **old** | **new** |

| | Unit 2 | Unit 2 | Unit 2 |
|---|---|---|---|
| **bee** | **ant** | **grasshopper** | **spider** |

| | Unit 2 | Unit 2 | Unit 2 |
|---|---|---|---|
| **ladybug** | **dragonfly** | **beetle** | **butterfly** |

Unit 1 short

Unit 1 long

Unit 1 small

Unit 1 big

Unit 1 cold

Unit 1 hot

Unit 1 old

Unit 1 new

Unit 2 bee

Unit 2 ant

Unit 2 grasshopper

Unit 2 spider

Unit 2 ladybug

Unit 2 dragonfly

Unit 2 beetle

Unit 2 butterfly

Unit 3

Unit 3

Unit 4

Unit 4

Unit 3

Unit 3

Unit 4

Unit 4

Unit 3

Unit 3

Unit 4

Unit 4

Unit 3

Unit 3

Unit 4

Unit 4

coat

boots

recorder

hat

sweater

piano

trumpet

vest

shoes

flute

guitar

scarf

shirt

violin

drums

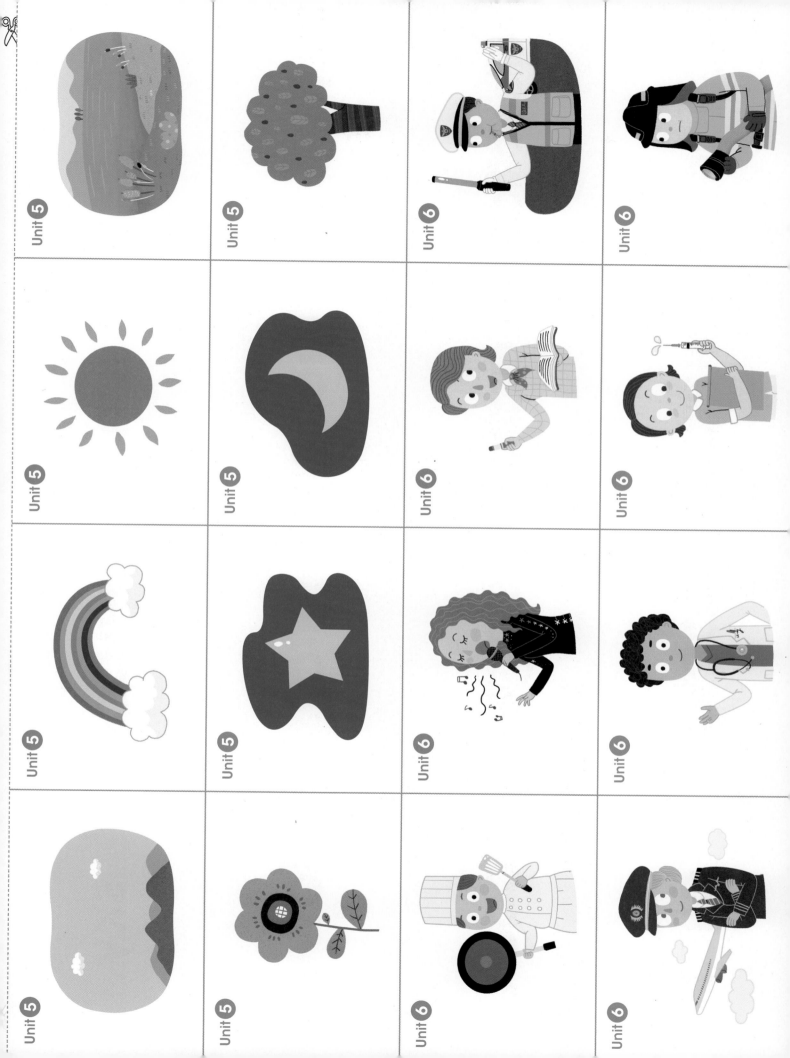

Unit 5

Unit 5

Unit 6

Unit 6

Unit 5

Unit 5

Unit 6

Unit 6

Unit 5

Unit 5

Unit 6

Unit 6

Unit 5

Unit 5

Unit 6

Unit 6

| Unit 5 | Unit 5 | Unit 5 | Unit 5 |
|---|---|---|---|
| lake | sun | rainbow | sky |

| Unit 5 | Unit 5 | Unit 5 | Unit 5 |
|---|---|---|---|
| tree | moon | star | flower |

| Unit 6 | Unit 6 | Unit 6 | Unit 6 |
|---|---|---|---|
| police officer | teacher | singer | cook |

| Unit 6 | Unit 6 | Unit 6 | Unit 6 |
|---|---|---|---|
| firefighter | nurse | doctor | pilot |

go

play

desk

eat

clean

table

bed

draw

help

wardrobe

bookcase

study

read

sofa

chair

# Midterm TEST 1c

Institute _____

Name _____

Score _____ /100

## [1-2] Listen and choose.
잘 듣고, 알맞은 그림을 고르세요.

**1** ⓐ   ⓑ

ⓒ   ⓓ

**2** ⓐ   ⓑ

ⓒ   ⓓ

## 3 Listen and choose.
잘 듣고, 그림에 알맞은 것을 고르세요.

  ⓐ  ⓑ  ⓒ  ⓓ

## [4-5] Listen and choose.
잘 듣고, 들려주는 단어들의 공통된 첫소리 글자를 고르세요.

**4** ⓐ p  ⓑ b

ⓒ t  ⓓ d

**5** ⓐ k  ⓑ g

ⓒ s  ⓓ z

## [6-7] Listen and choose.
잘 듣고, 빈칸에 알맞은 단어를 고르세요.

**6**  This is _____.

ⓐ big  ⓑ small

ⓒ new  ⓓ short

**7**  That's a _____.

ⓐ beetle  ⓑ dragonfly

ⓒ bee  ⓓ ladybug

## [8-9] Listen and choose.
잘 듣고, 그림에 알맞은 문장을 고르세요.

**8**    ⓐ  ⓑ  ⓒ  ⓓ

**9**    ⓐ  ⓑ  ⓒ  ⓓ

## 10 Listen and choose.
잘 듣고, 문장에 알맞은 그림을 고르세요.

ⓐ   ⓑ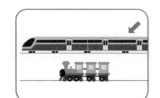

ⓒ   ⓓ

## Phonics

### [11-12] Look and choose.
그림을 보고, 주어진 단어와 첫소리가 같은 것을 고르세요.

**11**

p̲en

ⓐ   ⓑ

ⓒ   ⓓ

**12**

g̲irl

ⓐ   ⓑ

ⓒ   ⓓ

### [13-14] Look and choose.
그림을 보고, 빈칸에 알맞은 단어를 고르세요.

**13**

I like my red _____.

ⓐ shirt        ⓑ hat
ⓒ shoes        ⓓ vest

**14**

That's a _____.

ⓐ ladybug        ⓑ ant
ⓒ grasshopper    ⓓ butterfly

### 15 Read and mark ○ or ✕.
다음을 읽고, 그림과 일치하면 ○ 표, 일치하지 않으면 ✕ 표를 하세요.

This is old.

### [16-17] Look and choose.
그림을 보고, 알맞은 문장을 고르세요.

**16**

ⓐ I can play the drums.
ⓑ I can play the piano.
ⓒ I can play the flute.
ⓓ I can play the guitar.

**17**

ⓐ This is cold.
ⓑ This is big.
ⓒ This is long.
ⓓ This is small.

### [18-19] Look and write.
그림을 보고, 빈칸에 알맞은 말을 쓰세요.

**18**

I like my green _____.

**19**

That's a _____.

### 20 Unscramble.
단어를 배열하여 알맞은 문장을 만드세요.

( like / scarf / my / I / blue / . )

···▶ _____

# 🎧 Final TEST 1C

Institute _____

Name _____

Score _____ /100

## [1-2] Listen and choose.
잘 듣고, 그림에 해당하는 단어를 고르세요.

**1**   ⓐ   ⓑ   ⓒ   ⓓ

**2**   ⓐ   ⓑ   ⓒ   ⓓ

## [3-4] Listen and choose.
잘 듣고, 문장에 알맞은 그림을 고르세요.

**3** ⓐ    ⓑ

ⓒ    ⓓ

**4** ⓐ    ⓑ

ⓒ    ⓓ

**Phonics**

## [5-6] Listen and choose.
잘 듣고, 알맞은 첫소리의 알파벳을 고르세요.

**5** ⓐ f    ⓑ v    ⓒ m    ⓓ n

**6** ⓐ l    ⓑ r    ⓒ w    ⓓ y

## [7-8] Listen and choose.
잘 듣고, 빈칸에 알맞은 단어를 고르세요.

**7**

I'm a _____.

ⓐ police officer    ⓑ nurse
ⓒ firefighter    ⓓ doctor

**8**

Look at the _____.

ⓐ sky    ⓑ rainbow
ⓒ tree    ⓓ moon

## [9-10] Listen and choose.
잘 듣고, 빈칸에 알맞은 말을 고르세요.

**9**

A: Where's my truck?
B: _____

ⓐ    ⓑ    ⓒ    ⓓ

**10**

A: _____
B: Okay.

ⓐ    ⓑ    ⓒ    ⓓ

**Phonics**

## [11-12] Look and choose.
그림을 보고, 그림의 단어와 첫소리가 같은 것을 고르세요.

**11**

ⓐ <u>l</u>amp　　ⓑ <u>w</u>ing
ⓒ <u>r</u>abbit　　ⓓ <u>y</u>ogurt

**12**

ⓐ <u>f</u>ish　　ⓑ <u>v</u>an
ⓒ <u>m</u>ouse　　ⓓ <u>n</u>et

## [13-14] Look and choose.
그림을 보고, 알맞은 단어를 고르세요.

**13**

ⓐ sun　　ⓑ star
ⓒ rainbow　　ⓓ moon

**14**

ⓐ desk　　ⓑ bookcase
ⓒ table　　ⓓ bed

## 15 Look and choose.
그림을 보고, 빈칸에 알맞은 단어를 고르세요.

Let's _____.

ⓐ eat　　　　ⓑ clean
ⓒ read　　　　ⓓ play

## 16 Look and choose.
그림을 보고, 알맞은 문장을 고르세요.

ⓐ I'm a teacher.　　ⓑ I'm a singer.
ⓒ I'm a cook.　　ⓓ I'm a nurse.

## 17 Look and choose.
그림을 보고, 대화의 빈칸에 알맞은 말을 고르세요.

A: Where's my robot?
B: _____

ⓐ It's on the sofa.
ⓑ It's on the bed.
ⓒ It's on the wardrobe.
ⓓ It's on the chair.

## [18-19] Look and write.
그림을 보고, 빈칸에 알맞은 말을 쓰세요.

**18**

Look at the _____.

**19**

A: Let's _____.
B: Okay.

## 20 Unscramble and write.
단어를 배열하여 알맞은 문장을 만드세요.

A: Where's my ball?
B: ( on / It's / desk / the / .)

_____

# Let's Go · 1C

Unit **1** pp. 2~3

| big | hot | long | short |
|-----|-----|------|-------|
| old | new | cold | small |

p. 5

Unit **2** pp. 10~11

| an ant | a spider | a ladybug | a dragonfly |
|--------|----------|-----------|-------------|
| a bee | a beetle | a butterfly | a grasshopper |

p. 12

p. 15

Unit **3** pp. 20~21

| hat | coat | shoes | boots |
|-----|------|-------|-------|
| vest | shirt | scarf | sweater |

p. 22

**Unit 4** pp. 28~29

flute    violin    guitar    recorder
piano    drums    trumpet

**Unit 5** pp. 38~39

sun    star    tree    flower
sky    lake    moon    rainbow

p. 41

**Unit 6** pp. 46~47

cook    pilot    doctor    firefighter
nurse    singer    teacher    police officer

p. 51

| go | draw | help | clean |
| eat | read | play | study |

p. 58

Unit **8** pp. 64~65

| bed | desk | table | bookcase |
| sofa | chair | wardrobe | |

p. 66

p. 69

# LET'S GO

### to the English World

**1c**

# Word Book
# & Workbook

CHUNJAE EDUCATION, INC.

# Word Book

Let's GO to the English World 1c

2nd Edition

**A** **Listen and trace. Then say.** 02

①  **big**
큰

② 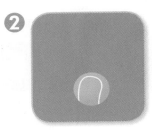 **small**
작은

③  **long**
긴

④  **short**
짧은

⑤  **new**
새로운

⑥  **old**
오래된

⑦  **hot**
뜨거운

⑧  **cold**
차가운

 **This is new.** 이것은 새 거야.

 **This is big.** 이것은 커.

**B Trace, write, and say.**

❶ 큰　　big

❷ 작은　　small

❸ 긴　　long

❹ 짧은　　short

❺ 새로운　　new

❻ 오래된　　old

❼ 뜨거운　　hot

❽ 차가운　　cold

**Listen and trace. Then say.** 15

①  **spider**
거미

②  **grasshopper**
메뚜기

③  **ant**
개미

④  **bee**
벌

⑤  **butterfly**
나비

⑥  **beetle**
딱정벌레

⑦  **dragonfly**
잠자리

⑧  **ladybug**
무당벌레

 **That's an ant.** 저것은 개미야.

 **That's a grasshopper.** 저것은 메뚜기야.

## B Trace, write, and say.

**❶ 거미**   spider

**❷ 메뚜기**   grasshopper

**❸ 개미**   ant

**❹ 벌**   bee

**❺ 나비**   butterfly

**❻ 딱정벌레**   beetle

**❼ 잠자리**   dragonfly

**❽ 무당벌레**   ladybug

## Ⓐ Listen and trace. Then say. 🎧29

①
**scarf**
스카프, 목도리

②
**hat**
(테가 있는) 모자

③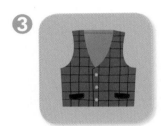
**vest**
조끼

④
**coat**
코트

⑤
**shirt**
셔츠

⑥
**sweater**
스웨터

⑦
**boots**
부츠

⑧
**shoes**
신발

**I like my** scarf. 나는 나의 스카프가 좋아.

**I like my** red scarf. 나는 나의 빨간색 스카프가 좋아.

6

**B** Trace, write, and say.

**1** 스카프,
목도리          scarf

**2** (테가 있는)
모자          hat

**3** 조끼          vest

**4** 코트          coat

**5** 셔츠          shirt

**6** 스웨터          sweater

**7** 부츠          boots

**8** 신발          shoes

# I Can Play the Piano

**A Listen and trace. Then say.** (42)

①  **violin**
바이올린

②  **flute**
플루트

③  **piano**
피아노

④ 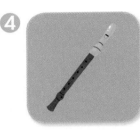 **recorder**
리코더

⑤  **drums**
드럼

⑥  **guitar**
기타

⑦  **trumpet**
트럼펫

 **I can play the** guitar. 나는 기타를 연주할 수 있어.

 **I can play the** piano. 나는 피아노를 연주할 수 있어.

**B** Trace, write, and say.

❶ 바이올린 violin

❷ 플루트 flute

❸ 피아노 piano

❹ 리코더 recorder

❺ 드럼 drums

❻ 기타 guitar

❼ 트럼펫 trumpet

# Look at the Lake

**Ⓐ Listen and trace. Then say.** 🎧56

❶  **sky**
하늘

❷  **rainbow**
무지개

❸  **sun**
해, 태양

❹  **lake**
호수

❺  **flower**
꽃

❻  **star**
별

❼  **moon**
달

❽  **tree**
나무

 **Look at the sun.** 해를 봐.

 **Look at the lake.** 호수를 봐.

**B** Trace, write, and say.

❶ 하늘 sky

❷ 무지개 rainbow

❸ 해, 태양 sun

❹ 호수 lake

❺ 꽃 flower

❻ 별 star

❼ 달 moon

❽ 나무 tree

# I'm a Police Officer

### A Listen and trace. Then say. 69

1
**cook**
요리사

2
**singer**
가수

3
**teacher**
선생님

4
**police officer**
경찰관

5
**pilot**
파일럿

6
**doctor**
의사

7
**nurse**
간호사

8
**firefighter**
소방관

**I'm a singer.** 나는 가수야.

**I'm a police officer.** 나는 경찰관이야.

**B** Trace, write, and say.

❶ 요리사    cook

❷ 가수     singer

❸ 선생님   teacher

❹ 경찰관   police officer

❺ 파일럿   pilot

❻ 의사     doctor

❼ 간호사   nurse

❽ 소방관   firefighter

## A Listen and trace. Then say. 83

①  **study**
공부하다

②  **draw**
그리다

③  **eat**
먹다

④  **go**
가다

⑤  **read**
읽다

⑥  **help**
돕다

⑦  **clean**
청소하다

⑧  **play**
놀다

 **Let's go.** 가자.

 **Okay.** 좋아.

**B** Trace, write, and say.

❶ 공부하다    study

❷ 그리다    draw

❸ 먹다    eat

❹ 가다    go

❺ 읽다    read

❻ 돕다    help

❼ 청소하다    clean

❽ 놀다    play

**Ⓐ Listen and trace. Then say.** 🎧96

①  **sofa**
소파

②  **wardrobe**
옷장

③  **table**
테이블, 탁자

④  **bookcase**
책장

⑤  **desk**
책상

⑥  **chair**
의자

⑦  **bed**
침대

 **Where's my robot?** 나의 로봇은 어디에 있니?

 **It's on the** sofa. 그것은 소파 위에 있어.

**B** Trace, write, and say.

❶ 소파     sofa

❷ 옷장     wardrobe

❸ 테이블,     table
    탁자

❹ 책장     bookcase

❺ 책상     desk

❻ 의자     chair

❼ 침대     bed

# Workbook

# This Is Big

# Learn

**A** Look and write.

| | | | |
|---|---|---|---|
| small | old | short | hot |
| big | new | cold | long |

1  _____

2  _____

3  _____

4  _____

5  _____

6  _____

7  _____

8  _____

## B Read and number.

1 This is big.　　2 This is long.　　3 This is cold.
4 This is new.　　5 This is small.　　6 This is short.
7 This is hot.　　8 This is old.

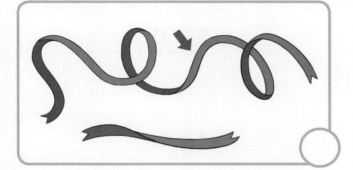 ○

 ○

 ○

 ○

 ○

 ○

 ○

 ○

# Let's Talk

## (A) Match and write.

**1**

This is • • o_____.

**2**

This is • • n_____.

**3**

This is • • b_____.

**4**

This is • • s_____.

## (B) Read and check.

**1** This is long.

**2** This is short.

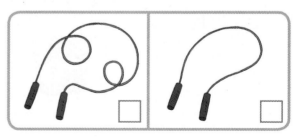

**3** This is hot.

**4** This is cold.

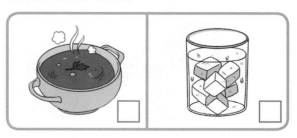

22

# Words

A Look and complete.

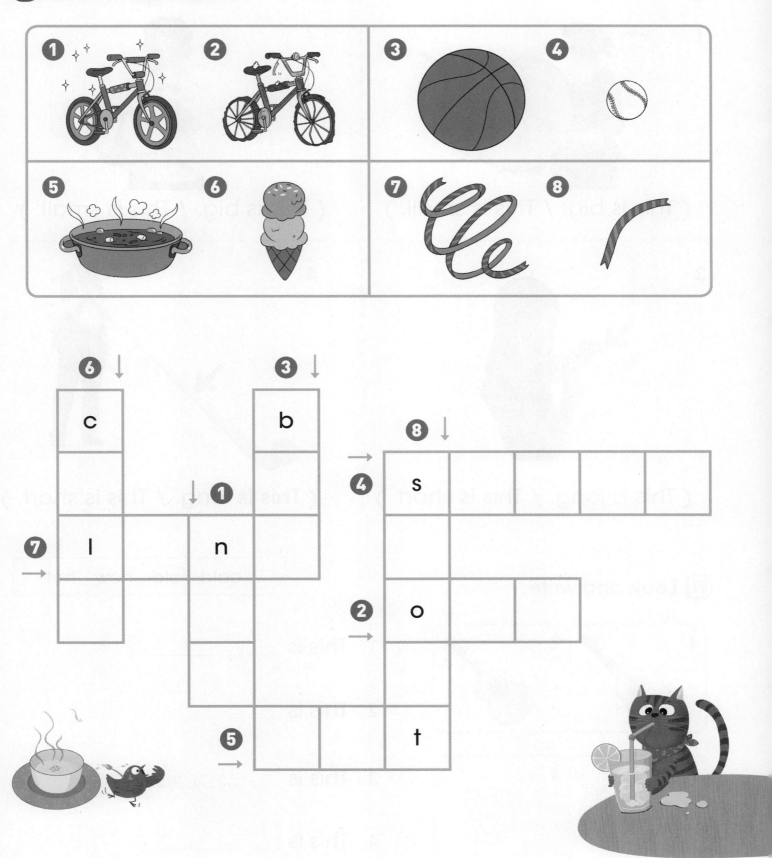

# Subject Link

## Ⓐ Read and circle.

**1**

( This is big. / This is small. )

**2**

( This is big. / This is small. )

**3**

( This is long. / This is short. )

**4**

( This is long. / This is short. )

## Ⓑ Look and write.

cold  old  new  hot

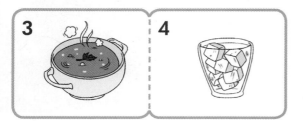

1  This is _____ .

2  This is _____ .

3  This is _____ .

4  This is _____ .

24

# Phonics

**Ⓐ Circle and write.**

1
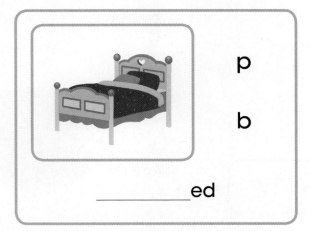

p

b

_____ed

2
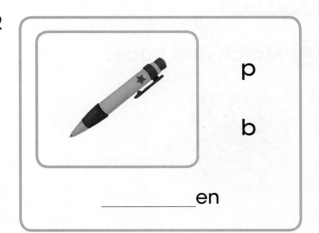

p

b

_____en

3

p

b

_____ig

4
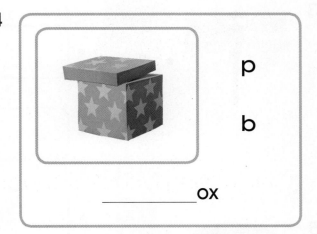

p

b

_____ox

5

p

b

_____ee

6
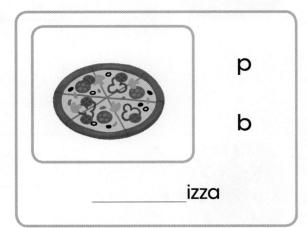

p

b

_____izza

# That's a Grasshopper

## Learn

Ⓐ Match and trace.

1

2

dragonfly

spider

3

4

bee

ant

beetle

5

6

grasshopper

butterfly

7

ladybug

8

**B** **Read and circle.**

1

That's
a bee.
a grasshopper.

2

That's
a beetle.
an ant.

3

That's
a ladybug.
an ant.

4

That's
a dragonfly.
a beetle.

5

That's
a bee.
a butterfly.

6

That's
a dragonfly.
a spider.

7

That's
a spider.
a butterfly.

8

That's
a ladybug.
a grasshopper.

# Let's Talk

**A** Read and number.

| | |
|---|---|
| 1 That's a grasshopper. | 2 That's a beetle. |
| 3 That's an ant. | 4 That's a butterfly. |
| 5 That's a bee. | 6 That's a ladybug. |
| 7 That's a dragonfly. | 8 That's a spider. |

28

# Words

**(A)** **Match and write.**

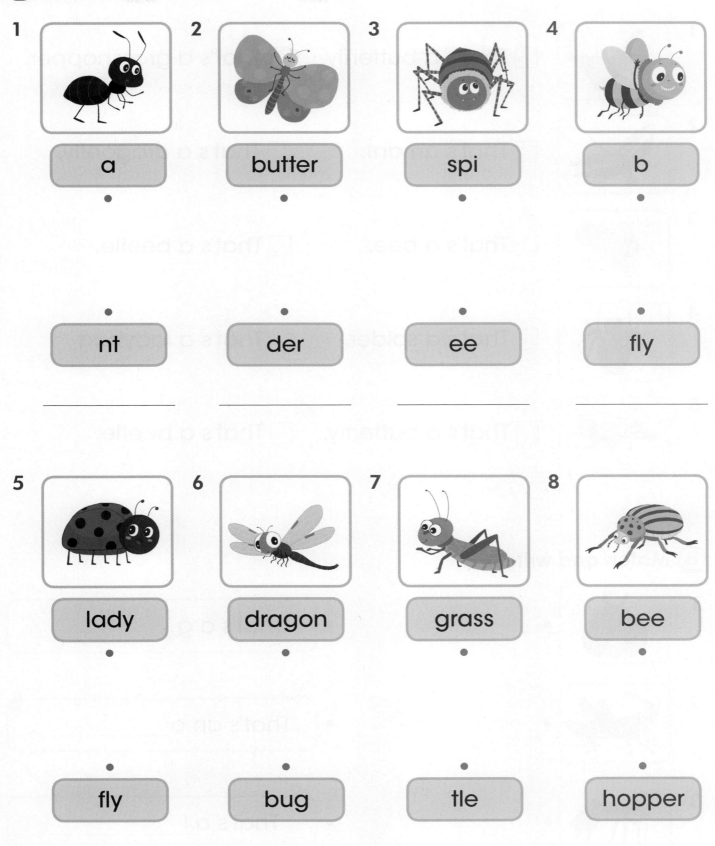

1
a

2
butter

3
spi

4
b

nt

der

ee

fly

5
lady

6
dragon

7
grass

8
bee

fly

bug

tle

hopper

# Subject Link

## Ⓐ Read and check.

**1** 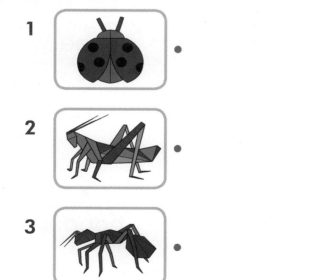  ☐ That's a butterfly.   ☐ That's a grasshopper.

**2**  ☐ That's an ant.   ☐ That's a dragonfly.

**3**  ☐ That's a bee.   ☐ That's a beetle.

**4**  ☐ That's a spider.   ☐ That's a ladybug.

**5**  ☐ That's a butterfly.   ☐ That's a beetle.

## Ⓑ Match and write.

**1**   •   •  That's a g_____.

**2**   •   •  That's an a_____.

**3**   •   •  That's a l_____.

# Phonics

**Ⓐ Look and write.**

1

_____urtle

2

_____esk

3

_____oll

4

_____ent

5

_____og

6

_____iger

| d | desk | | |
|---|------|---|---|
| t | turtle | | |

# I Like My Red Scarf

# Learn

## Ⓐ Trace and circle.

1
hat

2
sweater

3
coat

4
shirt

5
scarf

6
vest

7
shoes

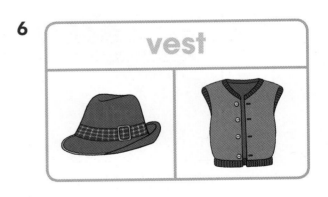

8
boots

## B Read, match, and color.

1  I like my yellow boots.  •

2  I like my green coat.  •

3  I like my red scarf.  •

4  I like my black shirt.  •

5  I like my blue shoes.  •

6  I like my white vest.  •

# Let's Talk

**A** Look and write.

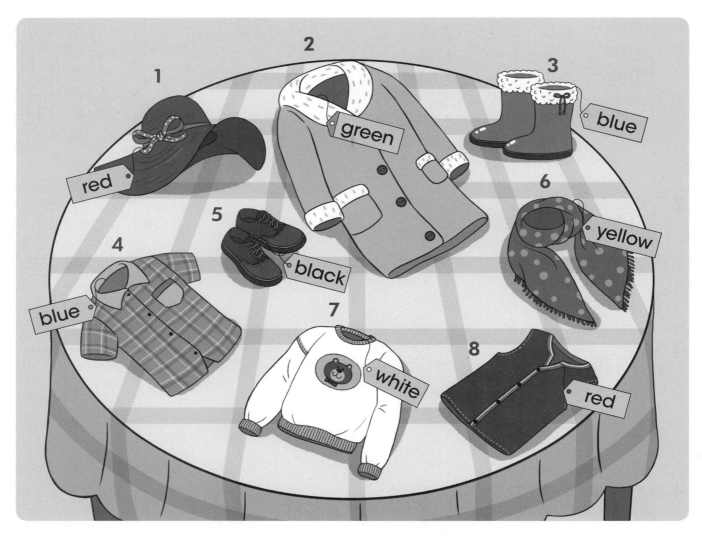

| coat | scarf | hat | vest |
|------|-------|-----|------|
| shirt | shoes | sweater | boots |

1  I like my _red hat_ .

2  I like my _____ .

3  I like my _____ .

4  I like my _____ .

5  I like my _____ .

6  I like my _____ .

7  I like my _____ .

8  I like my _____ .

# Words

**A** Unscramble and write.

1

i t r h s

_____

2

f s a c r

_____

3

o b t o s

_____

4

s s e h o

_____

5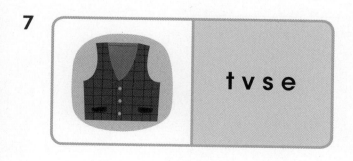

c t a o

_____

6

t e w a s r e

_____

7

t v s e

_____

8

a h t

_____

# Subject Link

## Ⓐ Read and circle.

**1**

I like my green
( shirt / shoes ).

**2**

I like my white
( sweater / scarf ).

**3**

I like my red
( shoes / scarf ).

**4**

I like my blue
( shoes / coat ).

## Ⓑ Look and write.

| boots | hat | sweater |

**1**

yellow

I like my _____ _____.

**2**

red

I like my _____ _____.

**3**

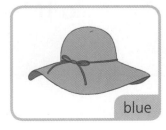

blue

I like my _____ _____.

# Phonics

**Ⓐ** Circle and match.

**1**

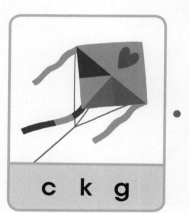

c  k  g

**2**

c  k  g

-ame

-ite

**3**

c  k  g

-oat

**4**

c  k  g

-at

**5**

c  k  g

-irl

**6**

c  k  g

# I Can Play the Piano

# Learn

**A** Look and write.

> recorder        trumpet        violin
> piano        flute        drums        guitar

1

_____

2

_____

3

_____

4

_____

5

_____

6

_____

7

_____

☐ I can play the recorder.  ☐ I can play the piano.

☐ I can play the drums.  ☐ I can play the flute.

☐ I can play the guitar.  ☐ I can play the violin.

# Let's Talk

## A Look and match.

1   I can play •      • the recorder.

2   I can play •      • the trumpet.

3     I can play •      • the violin.

4     I can play •      • the piano.

## B Read and check.

1

☐ I can play the flute.

☐ I can play the piano.

2

☐ I can play the guitar.

☐ I can play the drums.

# Words

**A** Circle and write.

**1**
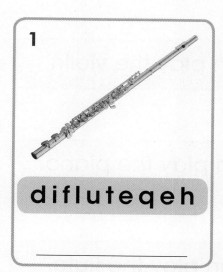
**difluteqeh**

_____

**2**
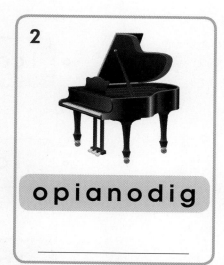
**opianodig**

_____

**3**

**eviolinegs**

_____

**4**

**ilfudrums**

_____

**5**

**guitareniu**

_____

**6**

**uprecorderes**

_____

**7**

**rytrumpetea**

_____

# Subject Link

**A** Read and match.

1

        I can play the trumpet.

2

        I can play the violin.

3

        I can play the piano.

4

        I can play the flute.

**B** Look and write.

drums   guitar   recorder

1

I can play the _____.

2

I can play the _____.

3

I can play the _____.

42

# Phonics

**Ⓐ Look and write s or z.**

1

_____oup

2

_____ebra

3

_____ero

4

_____un

5

_____ing

6

_____oo

# Look at the Lake

# Learn

## Ⓐ Read and circle.

**1** tree

**2** lake

**3** rainbow

**4** star

**5** sky

**6** flower

**7** sun

**8** moon

## B Look and complete.

**1**

Look at the l_____.

**2**

Look at the t_____.

**3**

Look at the r_____.

**4**

Look at the s_____.

**5**

Look at the m_____.

**6**

Look at the f_____.

**7**

Look at the s____.

**8**

Look at the s____.

# Let's Talk

## A Unscramble and write.

1

Look at the_____.
( r w l o f e )

2

Look at the_____.
( e t e r )

3

Look at the_____.
( k l e a )

4

Look at the_____.
( k y s )

## B Read and check.

1

Look at the star. ☐
Look at the moon. ☐

2

Look at the rainbow. ☐
Look at the flower. ☐

# Words

(A) Look and complete.

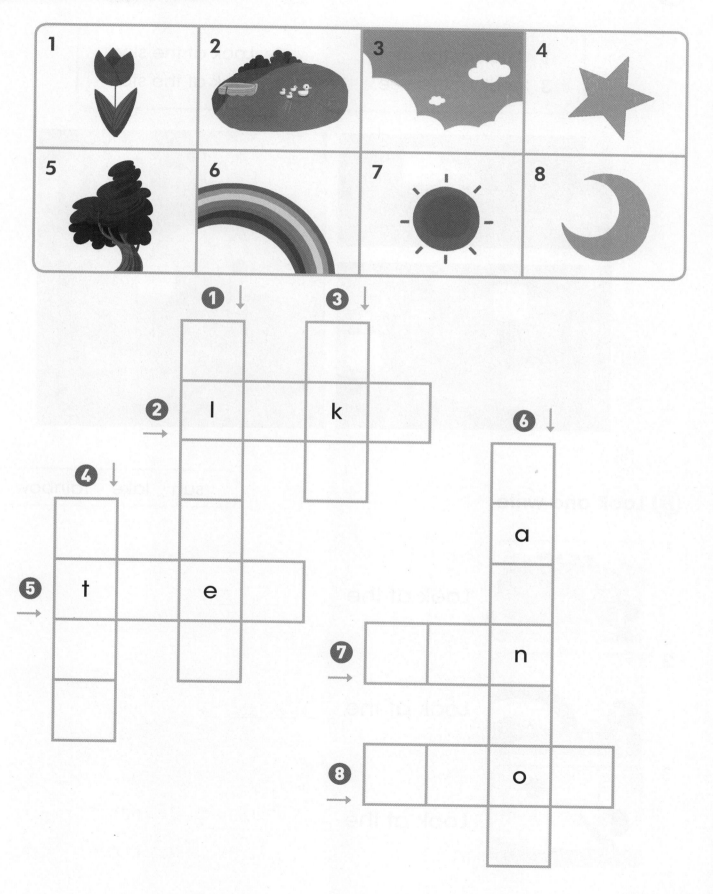

# Subject Link

**(A) Read and number.**

| | | | |
|---|---|---|---|
| **1** | Look at the moon. | **2** | Look at the sky. |
| **3** | Look at the tree. | **4** | Look at the star. |

**(B) Look and write.**

sun    lake    rainbow

**1**

Look at the _____.

**2**

Look at the _____.

**3**

Look at the _____.

# Phonics

## Ⓐ Circle and write.

**1**

f

v

_____ork

**2**

f

v

_____an

**3**

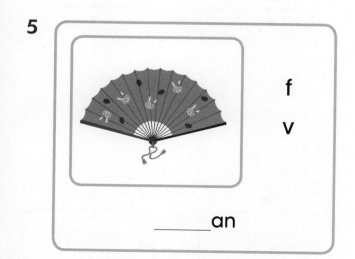

f

v

_____ish

**4**

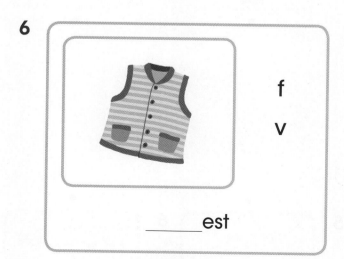

f

v

_____iolin

**5**

f

v

_____an

**6**

f

v

_____est

# Learn

**A** Match and trace.

1 firefighter

2 police officer

3 singer

4 doctor

5 nurse 6 teacher 7 cook 8 pilot

**B** Look and write.

| cook | doctor | singer | teacher |
| pilot | nurse | firefighter | police officer |

**1**

I'm a _____.

**2**

I'm a _____.

**3**

I'm a _____.

**4**

I'm a _____.

**5**

I'm a _____.

**6**

I'm a _____.

**7**

I'm a _____.

**8**

I'm a _____.

# Let's Talk

## A Write the letters and complete.

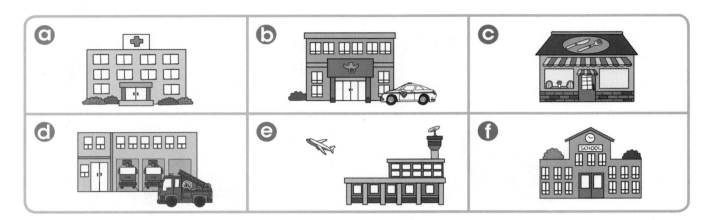

| 1 | 2 | 3 |
|---|---|---|
|  | |  |
| I'm a f_____ . | I'm a p_____ . | I'm a c_____ . |

| 4 | 5 | 6 |
|---|---|---|
|  | |  |
| I'm a t_____ . | I'm a p_____ . | I'm a d_____ . |

## B Look and circle.

1

I'm a ( singer / teacher ).

2

I'm a ( pilot / nurse ).

# Words

**A** Circle and write.

**1**

doctor

pilot

police officer

_____

**2**

firefighter

pilot

singer

_____

**3**

singer

teacher

nurse

_____

**4**

singer

firefighter

police officer

_____

**5**

cook

doctor

pilot

_____

**6**

teacher

cook

nurse

_____

**7**

doctor

police officer

firefighter

_____

**8**

nurse

cook

teacher

_____

# Subject Link

## Ⓐ Read and match.

1   I'm a teacher.   •

2   I'm a police officer.   •

3   I'm a firefighter.   •

4   I'm a doctor.   •

## Ⓑ Look and mark O or X.

1

I'm a nurse. ☐

2

I'm a pilot. ☐

# Phonics

## Ⓐ Match and write.

**1**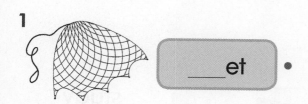
_____et •

**2**
_____onkey •

**3**
_____ose •

• **m**

**4**
_____ilk •

**5**
_____ine •

• **n**

**6**
_____ouse •

# Let's Go

# Learn

**Ⓐ Circle and write.**

1    go
draw

_____

2    study
play

_____

3    clean
help

_____

4    clean
study

_____

5    read
eat

_____

6    read
play

_____

7    help
eat

_____

8    go
draw

_____

**B** Read and circle.

1   Let's eat.

2   Let's play.

3   Let's read.

4   Let's go.

5   Let's draw.

6   Let's clean.

7   Let's study.

8   Let's help.

# Let's Talk

## A Look and match.

**1**

**2**

**3**

**4**

| Let's help. | Let's draw. | Let's study. | Let's clean. |
| Let's go. | Let's eat. | Let's play. | Let's read. |

**5**

**6**

**7**

**8**

# Words

**A** Find and circle. Then complete.

| w | e | r | p | l | a | y | p |
|---|---|---|---|---|---|---|---|
| y | a | s | d | s | e | h | g |
| m | t | t | f | v | d | j | o |
| t | d | u | h | r | e | a | d |
| h | n | d | m | c | a | q | z |
| e | a | y | d | r | a | w | c |
| l | e | x | l | o | k | f | b |
| p | r | c | l | e | a | n | i |

**1**

e___ ___

**2**

p___ ___y

**3** 

___e___p

**4**

___ ___

**5**

r___ ___d

**6**

___ra___

**7**

___ ___ea___

**8**

s___ ___ ___y

# Subject Link

## (A) Read and write the letters.

ⓐ   ⓑ  ⓒ   ⓓ

**1** | Let's play. | ☐
**3** | Let's eat. | ☐

**2** | Let's read. | ☐
**4** | Let's study. | ☐

## (B) Look and write.

| clean    go    help    draw |

**1**

Let's _____ .

**2**

Let's _____ .

**3**

Let's _____ .

**4**

Let's _____ .

# Phonics

## (A) Look and circle.

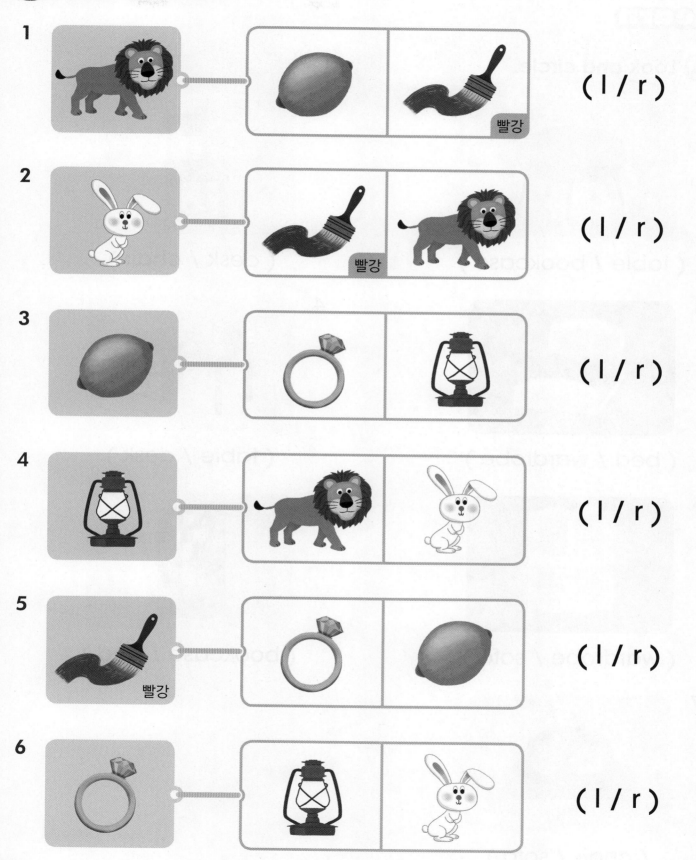

1  ( l / r )

2  ( l / r )

3  ( l / r )

4  ( l / r )

5  ( l / r )

6  ( l / r )

# UNIT 8 It's on the Sofa

# Learn

**A** Look and circle.

1

( table / bookcase )

2

( desk / chair )

3

( bed / wardrobe )

4

( table / desk )

5

( wardrobe / sofa )

6

( bookcase / bed )

7

( chair / sofa )

**B** Trace and match.

Where's my robot?

1  It's on the sofa. •

2  It's on the bookcase. •

3  It's on the wardrobe •

4  It's on the desk. •

5  It's on the bed. •

6  It's on the chair. •

7  It's on the table. •

# Let's Talk

**A** Read and number.

1
2
3
4

5
6
7

A: Where's my car?
B: It's on the bookcase. ☐

A: Where's my car?
B: It's on the sofa. ☐

A: Where's my car?
B: It's on the bed. ☐

A: Where's my car?
B: It's on the table. ☐

A: Where's my car?
B: It's on the chair. ☐

A: Where's my car?
B: It's on the desk. ☐

A: Where's my car?
B: It's on the wardrobe. ☐

# Words

**Ⓐ Cross out and write.**

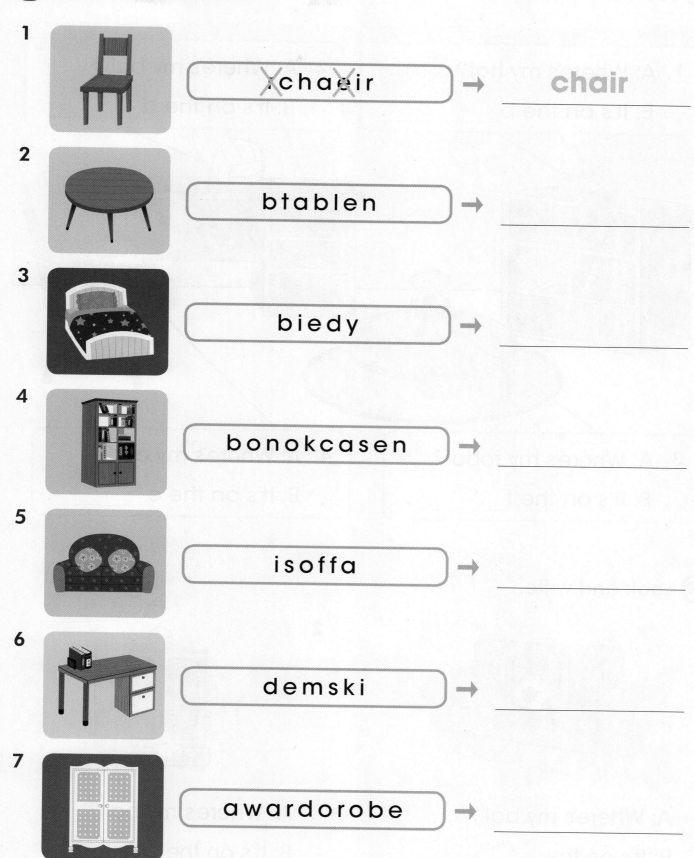

1. x cha x ir → **chair**

2. b table n →

3. b ied y →

4. b onokcase n →

5. i soffa →

6. demsk i →

7. awardorobe →

# Subject Link

**(A) Look and complete.**

1  A: Where's my hat?

B: It's on the b_____.

2  A: Where's my ball?

B: It's on the d_____.

3  A: Where's my robot?

B: It's on the t_____.

4  A: Where's my car?

B: It's on the c_____.

**(B) Look and write.**

1

A: Where's my ball?

B: It's on the _____.

2

A: Where's my ball?

B: It's on the _____.

# Phonics

**Ⓐ Look and write.**

1

_____olf

2

_____o-yo

3

_____ing

4

_____ogurt

5

노랑
_____ellow

6

_____ater

| w | y |
|---|---|
| wolf | |
| | |
| | |

**1c**